CATHOLIC PLANNER
2020-2021

_____

WELCOME

Welcome to the Catholic Planner Family! The Catholic Planner was created to help you accomplish all of your goals, stay organized, make time for yourself and your loved ones, and stay grounded in your faith throughout the year. We pray that this simple and effective tool will help you on your spiritual journey.

WHAT'S INSIDE?

Path to Sainthood: This beginning-of-the-year exercise is meant to help you reflect on the person that God is calling you to be. You will fill out each section of this chart to pinpoint your goals for 2020-2021, while ensuring that these goals align with God's will.

Monthly Calendar: These pages give you an overview of your whole month. You can find the liturgical calendar along with saint feast days and a saint of the month.

There is also space to brainstorm your goals for the month. This is a great way for you to kickstart your month and move forward with focus.

Weekly Retreat: Prepare spiritually for your week here. The readings for the upcoming Sunday's mass are provided for you and a snippet of the Gospel reading is featured. We encourage you to take out your bible to read all of the passages. Below the readings you are given space to reflect on the message you read.

The next section gives you space to write down how you were in awe of God throughout the week. This allows you to always be aware of God's presence in your life and highlight what you are grateful for.

The rituals and habits section helps you to get your life into a rhythm. You can list the rituals and habits you want to develop and check off the days you accomplish each one. Good daily habits are personal activities that are important to your own well-being (i.e. drinking 8 glasses of water, exercising, practicing a passion, etc.). Catholic rituals are religious activities that express your love for Christ (i.e. attending daily mass, attending a scripture study, performing acts of charity, etc.).

The prayer list helps you to add focus and structure to your communion with God.

Weekly Calendar: These pages give you space to organize your days by your school subjects. Use the boxes on the left to label the classes you have throughout the year.

MAKE IT YOUR OWN

There is no one right way to use the Catholic Planner. Discover the best way to use the Catholic Planner that is most effective for you. Put your personality into it and add some color. Make it your own!

KEEP IN TOUCH

For more tips on how to use the Catholic Planner visit us at CatholicPlanner.com. Follow us on Facebook at Facebook.com/CatholicPlanner and on Instagram and Twitter @CatholicPlanner. Share how you've personalized your Catholic Planner and tag us!

PATH TO SAINTHOOD GUIDE

Make this your best year ever by setting goals for yourself for the 2020-2021 school year! The Path to Sainthood helps you to look deep into what God's purpose is for you, so that you can come up with these goals.

> "Jesus, help me to simplify my life by learning what You want me to be and becoming that person."
> - Saint Therese of Lisieux -

INSTRUCTIONS

2019-2020 Achievements: Write down the achievements you were most proud of accomplishing last year - big or small.

God's Blessings: Reflect on the gifts that God has brought into your life. What are you most grateful for? What talents has He given you?

Inspiration: Write down the names of people who are inspirations in your life. These can be saints, friends, family, priests, teachers, or anyone else you can think of. Also write down the qualities and traits that make these people so inspirational.

Focus: Reflect on the categories in your life that you feel called to focus on, develop, work on, or maintain. Examples of these categories can be the Seven Virtues, the Fruit of the Spirit (Galatians 5:22-23), your family, your career, or your creativity.

2020-2021 Goals: After filling out the previous sections you should have a better idea of what is most important to you and what God is calling you to do or be. Set goals for yourself based on the direction given to you from your answers. Don't be afraid to dream big!

> "Be who God meant you to be and you will set the world on fire."
> - Saint Catherine of Siena -

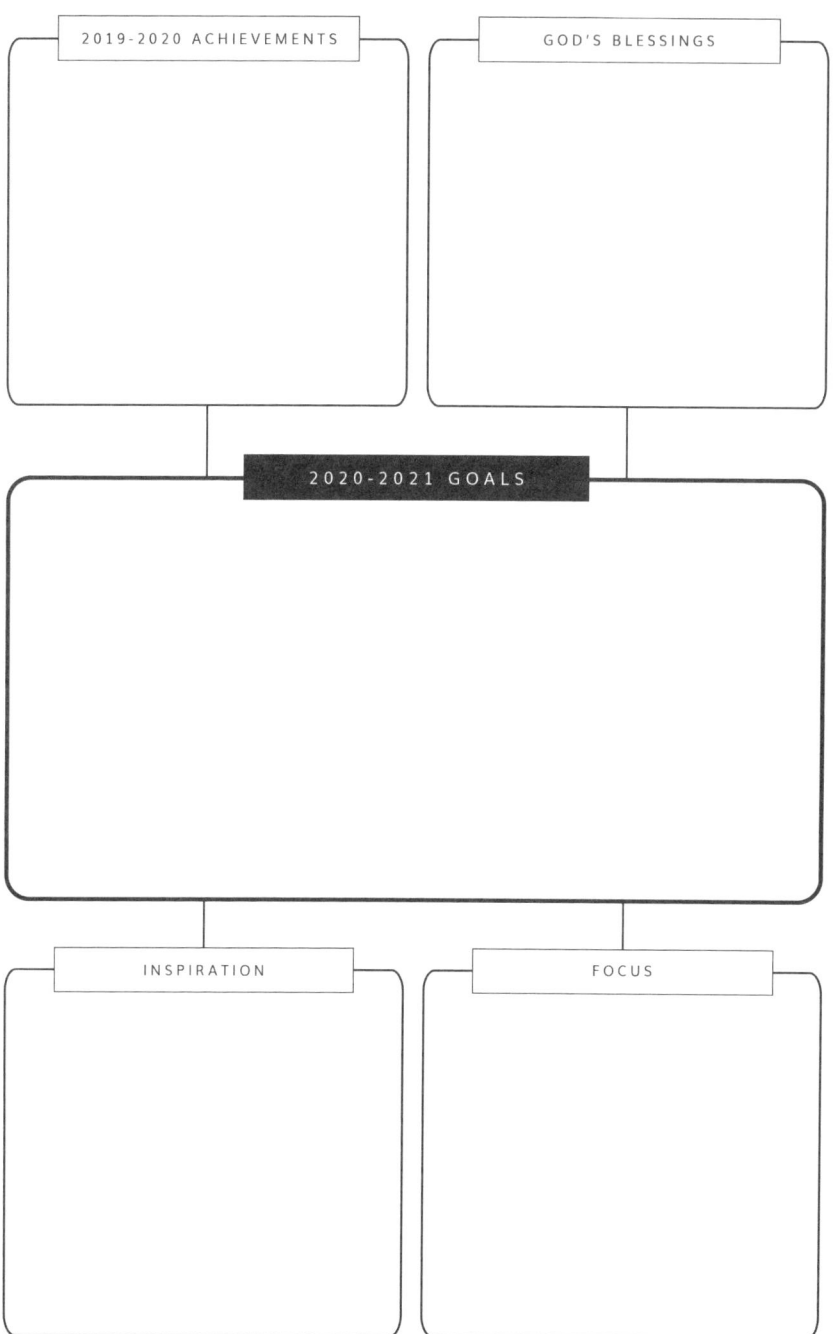

PATH TO SAINTHOOD

Use this space for brainstorming.

PATH TO SAINTHOOD

Use this space for brainstorming.

40 DAY LENTEN CHALLENGE

I WILL PREPARE FOR CHRIST'S DEATH & RESURRECTION BY

Brainstorm and choose what you feel called to commit to during the Lenten Season.

REFLECT

Why did you choose to commit to this?

MY SUPPORT TEAM

Who can help you along the way?

1	2	3	4	5	6	7	8	9	10	11	12	13	14	15	16	17	18	19	20
21	22	23	24	25	26	27	28	29	30	31	32	33	34	35	36	37	38	39	40

Initial after you complete each day.

2020-2021

AUGUST
S	M	T	W	T	F	S
						1
2	3	4	5	6	7	8
9	10	11	12	13	14	15
16	17	18	19	20	21	22
23	24	25	26	27	28	29
30	31					

SEPTEMBER
S	M	T	W	T	F	S
		1	2	3	4	5
6	7	8	9	10	11	12
13	14	15	16	17	18	19
20	21	22	23	24	25	26
27	28	29	30			

OCTOBER
S	M	T	W	T	F	S
				1	2	3
4	5	6	7	8	9	10
11	12	13	14	15	16	17
18	19	20	21	22	23	24
25	26	27	28	29	30	31

NOVEMBER
S	M	T	W	T	F	S
1	2	3	4	5	6	7
8	9	10	11	12	13	14
15	16	17	18	19	20	21
22	23	24	25	26	27	28
29	30					

DECEMBER
S	M	T	W	T	F	S
		1	2	3	4	5
6	7	8	9	10	11	12
13	14	15	16	17	18	19
20	21	22	23	24	25	26
27	28	29	30	31		

JANUARY
S	M	T	W	T	F	S
					1	2
3	4	5	6	7	8	9
10	11	12	13	14	15	16
17	18	19	20	21	22	23
24	25	26	27	28	29	30
31						

FEBRUARY
S	M	T	W	T	F	S
	1	2	3	4	5	6
7	8	9	10	11	12	13
14	15	16	17	18	19	20
21	22	23	24	25	26	27
28						

MARCH
S	M	T	W	T	F	S
	1	2	3	4	5	6
7	8	9	10	11	12	13
14	15	16	17	18	19	20
21	22	23	24	25	26	27
28	29	30	31			

APRIL
S	M	T	W	T	F	S
				1	2	3
4	5	6	7	8	9	10
11	12	13	14	15	16	17
18	19	20	21	22	23	24
25	26	27	28	29	30	

MAY
S	M	T	W	T	F	S
						1
2	3	4	5	6	7	8
9	10	11	12	13	14	15
16	17	18	19	20	21	22
23	24	25	26	27	28	29
30	31					

JUNE
S	M	T	W	T	F	S
		1	2	3	4	5
6	7	8	9	10	11	12
13	14	15	16	17	18	19
20	21	22	23	24	25	26
27	28	29	30			

JULY
S	M	T	W	T	F	S
				1	2	3
4	5	6	7	8	9	10
11	12	13	14	15	16	17
18	19	20	21	22	23	24
25	26	27	28	29	30	31

CLASS SCHEDULE

	MONDAY	TUESDAY	WEDNESDAY	THURSDAY	FRIDAY
5:00					
5:30					
6:00					
6:30					
7:00					
7:30					
8:00					
8:30					
9:00					
9:30					
10:00					
10:30					
11:00					
11:30					
12:00					
12:30					
1:00					
1:30					
2:00					
2:30					
3:00					
3:30					
4:00					
4:30					
5:00					
5:30					
6:00					
6:30					
7:00					
7:30					
8:00					
8:30					
9:00					
9:30					
10:00					

CLASS SCHEDULE

	MONDAY	TUESDAY	WEDNESDAY	THURSDAY	FRIDAY
5:00					
5:30					
6:00					
6:30					
7:00					
7:30					
8:00					
8:30					
9:00					
9:30					
10:00					
10:30					
11:00					
11:30					
12:00					
12:30					
1:00					
1:30					
2:00					
2:30					
3:00					
3:30					
4:00					
4:30					
5:00					
5:30					
6:00					
6:30					
7:00					
7:30					
8:00					
8:30					
9:00					
9:30					
10:00					

CLASS SCHEDULE

	MONDAY	TUESDAY	WEDNESDAY	THURSDAY	FRIDAY
5:00					
5:30					
6:00					
6:30					
7:00					
7:30					
8:00					
8:30					
9:00					
9:30					
10:00					
10:30					
11:00					
11:30					
12:00					
12:30					
1:00					
1:30					
2:00					
2:30					
3:00					
3:30					
4:00					
4:30					
5:00					
5:30					
6:00					
6:30					
7:00					
7:30					
8:00					
8:30					
9:00					
9:30					
10:00					

CLASS SCHEDULE

	MONDAY	TUESDAY	WEDNESDAY	THURSDAY	FRIDAY
5:00					
5:30					
6:00					
6:30					
7:00					
7:30					
8:00					
8:30					
9:00					
9:30					
10:00					
10:30					
11:00					
11:30					
12:00					
12:30					
1:00					
1:30					
2:00					
2:30					
3:00					
3:30					
4:00					
4:30					
5:00					
5:30					
6:00					
6:30					
7:00					
7:30					
8:00					
8:30					
9:00					
9:30					
10:00					

AUGUST

NOTES

SUNDAY	MONDAY	TUESDAY
2 — Eighteenth Sunday in Ordinary Time	3 — Civic Holiday (CA)	4
9 — Nineteenth Sunday in Ordinary Time	10 — Saint Lawrence	11 — Saint Clare
16 — Twentieth Sunday in Ordinary Time	17	18
23 — Twenty-First Sunday in Ordinary Time	24 — Saint Bartholomew	25
30 — Twenty-Second Sunday in Ordinary Time	31	Saint Louis / Saint Joseph Calasanz

SAINT JANE FRANCES DE CHANTAL

- Feast Day: August 21
- Born: January 28, 1572; Died: December 31, 1641
- Patron saint of forgotten people, loss of parents, parents separated from children and widows
- Saint Jane Frances de Chantal was left a widow at the age of 28 when her husband was shot and killed in a hunting accident by his friend.
- She struggled with forgiveness, but eventually forgave the man and later became godmother to his child.
- She founded the Congregation of the Visitation, which accepted women who were rejected because of their poor health or age.
- It grew to 13 houses by the time of her death.

WEDNESDAY	THURSDAY	FRIDAY	SATURDAY
			1 Saint Alphonsus Liguori
5 The Dedication of the Basilica of Saint Mary Major	6 The Transfiguration of the Lord	7	8 Saint Dominic
12	13 Saints Pontian and Hippolytus	14 Saint Maximilian Kolbe	15 The Assumption of the Blessed Virgin Mary
19 Saint John Eudes	20 Saints Bernard	21 Saint Pius X Saint Jane Frances de Chantal	22 The Queenship of the Blessed Virgin Mary
26	27 Saint Monica	28 Saint Augustine	29 The Passion of Saint John the Baptist

GOALS

WEEKLY RETREAT • AUGUST 2, 2020

READING 1	READING 2	GOSPEL
Isaiah 55:1-3	Romans 8:35, 37-39	Matthew 14:13-21

When it was evening, the disciples approached him and said, "This is a deserted place and it is already late; dismiss the crowds so that they can go to the villages and buy food for themselves." [Jesus] said to them, "There is no need for them to go away; give them some food yourselves."

Matthew 14:15-16

REFLECTION

HOW WERE YOU IN AWE OF GOD THIS WEEK?

WEEKLY RETREAT

FREE SPACE

HABITS & RITUALS

M	T	W	T	F	S	S
M	T	W	T	F	S	S
M	T	W	T	F	S	S
M	T	W	T	F	S	S
M	T	W	T	F	S	S

PRAYER LIST

JUL & AUG

27 MONDAY	28 TUESDAY	29 WEDNESDAY

NOTES

30 THURSDAY	31 FRIDAY	PRIORITIES

TO DO LIST

- [ ]
- [ ]
- [ ]
- [ ]
- [ ]
- [ ]
- [ ]
- [ ]
- [ ]
- [ ]
- [ ]
- [ ]
- [ ]
- [ ]
- [ ]
- [ ]
- [ ]
- [ ]
- [ ]
- [ ]
- [ ]

1 SATURDAY	2 SUNDAY

WEEKLY RETREAT • AUGUST 9, 2020

READING 1	READING 2	GOSPEL
1 Kings 19:9a, 11-13a	Romans 9:1-5	Matthew 14:22-33

During the fourth watch of the night, he came toward them, walking on the sea. When the disciples saw him walking on the sea they were terrified. "It is a ghost," they said, and they cried out in fear. At once [Jesus] spoke to them, "Take courage, it is I; do not be afraid."

Matthew 14:25-27

REFLECTION

HOW WERE YOU IN AWE OF GOD THIS WEEK?

WEEKLY RETREAT

FREE SPACE

HABITS & RITUALS

M	T	W	T	F	S	S
M	T	W	T	F	S	S
M	T	W	T	F	S	S
M	T	W	T	F	S	S
M	T	W	T	F	S	S

PRAYER LIST

8 AUGUST

MONDAY 3	TUESDAY 4	WEDNESDAY 5
Civic Holiday (CA)		

NOTES

THURSDAY 6	FRIDAY 7	PRIORITIES

TO DO LIST

SATURDAY 8	SUNDAY 9

WEEKLY RETREAT • AUGUST 16, 2020

READING 1	READING 2	GOSPEL
Isaiah 56:1, 6-7	Romans 11:13-15, 29-32	Matthew 15:21-28

But the woman came and did him homage, saying, "Lord, help me." He said in reply, "It is not right to take the food of the children and throw it to the dogs." She said, "Please, Lord, for even the dogs eat the scraps that fall from the table of their masters."

Matthew 15:25-27

REFLECTION

HOW WERE YOU IN AWE OF GOD THIS WEEK?

WEEKLY RETREAT

FREE SPACE

HABITS & RITUALS

M	T	W	T	F	S	S
M	T	W	T	F	S	S
M	T	W	T	F	S	S
M	T	W	T	F	S	S
M	T	W	T	F	S	S

PRAYER LIST

AUGUST

10 MONDAY	11 TUESDAY	12 WEDNESDAY

NOTES

THURSDAY 13

FRIDAY 14

PRIORITIES

TO DO LIST

SATURDAY 15
The Assumption of the Blessed Virgin Mary

SUNDAY 16

WEEKLY RETREAT • AUGUST 23, 2020

READING 1	READING 2	GOSPEL
Isaiah 22:19-23	Romans 11:33-36	Matthew 16:13-20

And so I say to you, you are Peter, and upon this rock I will build my church, and the gates of the netherworld shall not prevail against it. I will give you the keys to the kingdom of heaven. Whatever you bind on earth shall be bound in heaven; and whatever you loose on earth shall be loosed in heaven."

Matthew 16:18-19

REFLECTION

HOW WERE YOU IN AWE OF GOD THIS WEEK?

WEEKLY RETREAT

FREE SPACE

HABITS & RITUALS							PRAYER LIST
M	T	W	T	F	S	S	
M	T	W	T	F	S	S	
M	T	W	T	F	S	S	
M	T	W	T	F	S	S	
M	T	W	T	F	S	S	

8 AUGUST

17 MONDAY	18 TUESDAY	19 WEDNESDAY

NOTES

THURSDAY 20	FRIDAY 21	PRIORITIES

TO DO LIST

- [ ]
- [ ]
- [ ]
- [ ]
- [ ]
- [ ]
- [ ]
- [ ]
- [ ]
- [ ]
- [ ]
- [ ]
- [ ]
- [ ]
- [ ]
- [ ]
- [ ]
- [ ]
- [ ]
- [ ]
- [ ]
- [ ]
- [ ]

SATURDAY 22	SUNDAY 23

WEEKLY RETREAT • AUGUST 30, 2020

READING 1	READING 2	GOSPEL
Jeremiah 20:7-9	Romans 12:1-2	Matthew 16:21-27

Then Jesus said to his disciples, "Whoever wishes to come after me must deny himself, take up his cross, and follow me. For whoever wishes to save his life will lose it, but whoever loses his life for my sake will find it.

Matthew 16:24-25

REFLECTION

HOW WERE YOU IN AWE OF GOD THIS WEEK?

WEEKLY RETREAT

FREE SPACE

HABITS & RITUALS	PRAYER LIST
M T W T F S S	
M T W T F S S	
M T W T F S S	
M T W T F S S	
M T W T F S S	

8 AUGUST

24 MONDAY	25 TUESDAY	26 WEDNESDAY

NOTES

THURSDAY 27	FRIDAY 28	PRIORITIES

TO DO LIST

SATURDAY 29	SUNDAY 30

SEPTEMBER

NOTES

SUNDAY	MONDAY	TUESDAY
		1
6 — Twenty-Third Sunday in Ordinary Time	7 — Labor Day	8 — The Nativity of the Blessed Virgin Mary
13 — Twenty-Fourth Sunday in Ordinary Time	14 — The Exaltation of the Holy Cross	15 — Our Lady of Sorrows
20 — Twenty-Fifth Sunday in Ordinary Time	21 — Saint Matthew	22
27 — Twenty-Sixth Sunday in Ordinary Time	28 — Saint Wenceslaus; Saint Lawrence Ruiz & Companions	29 — Saints Michael, Gabriel, & Raphael

SAINT WENCESLAUS

- Feast Day: September 28
- Born: c.907; Died: September 28, 935
- Patron saint of Prague, Bohemia, Czech Republic
- Saint Wenceslaus was the son of Vratislaus I, Duke of Bohemia, and Drahomíra, the daughter of a pagan chief.
- His grandmother educated him in Catholic Faith.
- When his father died, Drahomíra took the role of regent and enacted policies against Christians.
- Christian nobles fought and succeeded in putting Wenceslaus into power when he turned 18.
- To prevent disputes, the country was divided between Wenceslaus and his brother, Boleslav.
- Boleslav had Wenceslaus stabbed to death.

WEDNESDAY	THURSDAY	FRIDAY	SATURDAY
2 *Labour Day (CA)*	3 Saint Gregory the Great	4	5
9 Saint Peter Claver	10	11	12 The Most Holy Name of Mary
16 Saints Cornelius & Cyprian	17 Saint Robert Bellarmine	18	19 Saint Januarius
23 Saint Pius of Pietrelcina	24	25	26 Saints Cosmas & Damian
30 Saint Jerome			

GOALS

WEEKLY RETREAT • SEPTEMBER 6, 2020

READING 1	READING 2	GOSPEL
Ezekiel 33:7-9	Romans 13:8-10	Matthew 18:15-20

Again, [amen,] I say to you, if two of you agree on earth about anything for which they are to pray, it shall be granted to them by my heavenly Father. For where two or three are gathered together in my name, there am I in the midst of them."

Matthew 18:19-20

REFLECTION

HOW WERE YOU IN AWE OF GOD THIS WEEK?

WEEKLY RETREAT

FREE SPACE

HABITS & RITUALS

M	T	W	T	F	S	S
M	T	W	T	F	S	S
M	T	W	T	F	S	S
M	T	W	T	F	S	S
M	T	W	T	F	S	S

PRAYER LIST

AUG & SEP

MONDAY 31	TUESDAY 1	WEDNESDAY 2
		Labour Day (CA)

NOTES

3 THURSDAY	4 FRIDAY	PRIORITIES

TO DO LIST

5 SATURDAY	6 SUNDAY

WEEKLY RETREAT • SEPTEMBER 13, 2020

READING 1	READING 2	GOSPEL
Sirach 27:30—28:7	Romans 14:7-9	Matthew 18:21-35

Then Peter approaching asked him, "Lord, if my brother sins against me, how often must I forgive him? As many as seven times?" Jesus answered, "I say to you, not seven times but seventy-seven times.

Matthew 18:21-22

REFLECTION

HOW WERE YOU IN AWE OF GOD THIS WEEK?

WEEKLY RETREAT

FREE SPACE

HABITS & RITUALS

M	T	W	T	F	S	S
M	T	W	T	F	S	S
M	T	W	T	F	S	S
M	T	W	T	F	S	S
M	T	W	T	F	S	S

PRAYER LIST

SEPTEMBER

7 MONDAY	8 TUESDAY	9 WEDNESDAY
Labor Day		

NOTES

THURSDAY 10	FRIDAY 11	PRIORITIES

TO DO LIST

SATURDAY 12	SUNDAY 13

WEEKLY RETREAT • SEPTEMBER 20, 2020

READING 1	READING 2	GOSPEL
Isaiah 55:6-9	Philippians 1:20c-24, 27a	Matthew 20:1-16a

"The kingdom of heaven is like a landowner who went out at dawn to hire laborers for his vineyard. After agreeing with them for the usual daily wage, he sent them into his vineyard. Going out about nine o'clock, he saw others standing idle in the marketplace, and he said to them, 'You too go into my vineyard, and I will give you what is just.'

Matthew 20:1-4

REFLECTION

HOW WERE YOU IN AWE OF GOD THIS WEEK?

WEEKLY RETREAT

FREE SPACE

HABITS & RITUALS

M	T	W	T	F	S	S
M	T	W	T	F	S	S
M	T	W	T	F	S	S
M	T	W	T	F	S	S
M	T	W	T	F	S	S

PRAYER LIST

9 SEPTEMBER

14 MONDAY	15 TUESDAY	16 WEDNESDAY

NOTES

17 THURSDAY	18 FRIDAY	PRIORITIES

TO DO LIST

19 SATURDAY	20 SUNDAY

WEEKLY RETREAT • SEPTEMBER 27, 2020

READING 1	READING 2	GOSPEL
Ezekiel 18:25-28	Philippians 2:1-11 or 2:1-5	Matthew 21:28-32

"What is your opinion? A man had two sons. He came to the first and said, 'Son, go out and work in the vineyard today.' He said in reply, 'I will not,' but afterwards he changed his mind and went. The man came to the other son and gave the same order. He said in reply, 'Yes, sir,' but did not go.

Matthew 21:28-30

REFLECTION

HOW WERE YOU IN AWE OF GOD THIS WEEK?

WEEKLY RETREAT

FREE SPACE

HABITS & RITUALS

M	T	W	T	F	S	S
M	T	W	T	F	S	S
M	T	W	T	F	S	S
M	T	W	T	F	S	S
M	T	W	T	F	S	S

PRAYER LIST

9 SEPTEMBER

MONDAY 21 | TUESDAY 22 | WEDNESDAY 23

NOTES

24 THURSDAY	25 FRIDAY	PRIORITIES

TO DO LIST

26 SATURDAY	27 SUNDAY

OCTOBER

SUNDAY	MONDAY	TUESDAY
4 Twenty-Seventh Sunday in Ordinary Time	**5** *Blessed Francis Xavier Seelos*	**6** *Saint Bruno*
11 Twenty-Eighth Sunday in Ordinary Time	**12** *Columbus Day/ Indigenous Peoples' Day* *Thanksgiving (CA)*	**13**
18 Twenty-Ninth Sunday in Ordinary Time	**19** *Saints John de Brébeuf & Isaac Jogues & Companions*	**20** *Saint Paul of the Cross*
25 Thirtieth Sunday in Ordinary Time	**26**	**27**

NOTES

SAINT BRUNO

- Feast Day: October 6
- Born: c.1030; Died: October 6, 1101
- Patron saint of Germany, Calabria, monastic fraternities, trade marks and possessed people
- Saint Bruno studied theology in the present-day French city of Reims, then went back to Cologne.
- He returned to Reims to teach theology.
- The following year, Bruno became head of the school for almost two decades.
- Bruno was set to become archbishop of Reims, but he decided to pursue a life of solitary in which he and his group prayed and studied in poverty.
- Pope Urban II, whom Bruno had taught, brought him to Rome to become Papal adviser.

WEDNESDAY	THURSDAY	FRIDAY	SATURDAY
	1 Saint Thérèse of the Child Jesus	2 The Holy Guardian Angels	3
7 Our Lady of the Rosary	8	9 Saint Denis Saint John Leonardi	10
14 Saint Callistus I	15 Saint Teresa of Jesus	16 Saint Hedwig Saint Margaret Mary Alacoque	17 Saint Ignatius of Antioch
21	22 Saint John Paul II	23 Saint John of Capistrano	24 Saint Anthony Mary Claret
28 Saints Simon & Jude	29	30	31

GOALS

WEEKLY RETREAT • OCTOBER 4, 2020

READING 1	READING 2	GOSPEL
Isaiah 5:1-7	Philippians 4:6-9	Matthew 21:33-43

Jesus said to them, "Did you never read in the scriptures: 'The stone that the builders rejected has become the cornerstone; by the Lord has this been done, and it is wonderful in our eyes'? Therefore, I say to you, the kingdom of God will be taken away from you and given to a people that will produce its fruit.

Matthew 21:42-43

REFLECTION

HOW WERE YOU IN AWE OF GOD THIS WEEK?

WEEKLY RETREAT

FREE SPACE

HABITS & RITUALS

M	T	W	T	F	S	S
M	T	W	T	F	S	S
M	T	W	T	F	S	S
M	T	W	T	F	S	S
M	T	W	T	F	S	S

PRAYER LIST

SEP & OCT

MONDAY 28	TUESDAY 29	WEDNESDAY 30

NOTES

1 THURSDAY	2 FRIDAY	PRIORITIES

TO DO LIST

3 SATURDAY	4 SUNDAY

WEEKLY RETREAT • OCTOBER 11, 2020

READING 1	READING 2	GOSPEL
Isaiah 25:6-10a	Philippians 4:12-14, 19-20	Matthew 22:1-14

Then he said to his servants, 'The feast is ready, but those who were invited were not worthy to come. Go out, therefore, into the main roads and invite to the feast whomever you find.' The servants went out into the streets and gathered all they found, bad and good alike, and the hall was filled with guests.

Matthew 22:8-10

REFLECTION

HOW WERE YOU IN AWE OF GOD THIS WEEK?

WEEKLY RETREAT

FREE SPACE

HABITS & RITUALS	PRAYER LIST

M T W T F S S

M T W T F S S

M T W T F S S

M T W T F S S

M T W T F S S

10 OCTOBER

5 MONDAY	6 TUESDAY	7 WEDNESDAY

NOTES

THURSDAY 8	FRIDAY 9	PRIORITIES

TO DO LIST

SATURDAY 10	SUNDAY 11

WEEKLY RETREAT • OCTOBER 18, 2020

READING 1	READING 2	GOSPEL
Isaiah 45:1, 4-6	1 Thessalonians 1:1-5b	Matthew 22:15-21

Tell us, then, what is your opinion: Is it lawful to pay the census tax to Caesar or not?" Knowing their malice, Jesus said, "Why are you testing me, you hypocrites? Show me the coin that pays the census tax." Then they handed him the Roman coin.

Matthew 22:17-19

REFLECTION

HOW WERE YOU IN AWE OF GOD THIS WEEK?

WEEKLY RETREAT

FREE SPACE

HABITS & RITUALS

M	T	W	T	F	S	S
M	T	W	T	F	S	S
M	T	W	T	F	S	S
M	T	W	T	F	S	S
M	T	W	T	F	S	S

PRAYER LIST

10 OCTOBER

MONDAY 12
Columbus Day
Indigenous Peoples' Day
Thanksgiving (CA)

TUESDAY 13

WEDNESDAY 14

NOTES

THURSDAY 15

FRIDAY 16

PRIORITIES

TO DO LIST

SATURDAY 17

SUNDAY 18

WEEKLY RETREAT • OCTOBER 25, 2020

READING 1	READING 2	GOSPEL
Exodus 22:20-26	1 Thessalonians 1:5c-10	Matthew 22:34-40

"Teacher, which commandment in the law is the greatest?" He said to him, "You shall love the Lord, your God, with all your heart, with all your soul, and with all your mind. This is the greatest and the first commandment.

Matthew 22:36-38

REFLECTION

HOW WERE YOU IN AWE OF GOD THIS WEEK?

WEEKLY RETREAT

FREE SPACE

HABITS & RITUALS

M	T	W	T	F	S	S
M	T	W	T	F	S	S
M	T	W	T	F	S	S
M	T	W	T	F	S	S
M	T	W	T	F	S	S

PRAYER LIST

10 OCTOBER

19 MONDAY	20 TUESDAY	21 WEDNESDAY

NOTES

22 THURSDAY	23 FRIDAY	PRIORITIES

TO DO LIST

24 SATURDAY	25 SUNDAY

NOVEMBER

NOTES

SUNDAY	MONDAY	TUESDAY
1 All Saints	**2** All Souls' Day	**3** Election Day Saint Martin de Porres
8 Thirty-Second Sunday in Ordinary Time	**9** The Dedication of the Lateran Basilica	**10** Saint Leo the Great
15 Thirty-Third Sunday in Ordinary Time	**16** Saint Margaret of Scotland Saint Gertrude	**17** Saint Elizabeth of Hungary
22 Our Lord Jesus Christ, King of the Universe Saint Cecilia	**23** Saint Clemont I Saint Columban Blessed Miguel Agustin Pro	**24** Saint Andrew Dũng-Lạc & Companions
29 First Sunday of Advent	**30** Saint Andrew	

SAINT CECILIA

- Feast Day: November 22
- Born: 2nd century AD; Died: 176-180 or 222-235
- Patron saint of hymns, musicians, and poets
- She was forced to marry a pagan nobleman named Valerian.
- During the wedding, she sat apart singing to God.
- She vowed virginity.
- On their wedding night, Cecilia told Valerian that an angel of the Lord was protecting her. Valerian asked for proof, so Cecilia said he would see after he is baptised by Pope Urban I. Valerian returned after his baptism and saw the angel with Cecilia.
- Cecilia was arrested and ordered to death.
- She was unable to be decapitated.

WEDNESDAY	THURSDAY	FRIDAY	SATURDAY
4 Saint Charles Borromeo	5	6	7
11 *Veterans Day* *Remembrance Day (CA)* Saint Martin of Tours	12 Saint Josaphat	13 Saint Frances Xavier Cabrini	14
18 The Dedication of the Basilicas of Saints Peter & Paul Saint Rose Philippine Duchesne	19	20	21 The Presentation of the Blessed Virgin Mary
25 Saint Catherine of Alexandria	26 *Thanksgiving*	27	28

GOALS

WEEKLY RETREAT • NOVEMBER 1, 2020

READING 1	READING 2	GOSPEL
Revelation 7:2-4, 9-14	1 John 3:1-3	Matthew 5:1-12a

Blessed are you when they insult you and persecute you and utter every kind of evil against you [falsely] because of me. Rejoice and be glad, for your reward will be great in heaven. Thus they persecuted the prophets who were before you.

Matthew 5:11-12

REFLECTION

HOW WERE YOU IN AWE OF GOD THIS WEEK?

WEEKLY RETREAT

FREE SPACE

HABITS & RITUALS

M	T	W	T	F	S	S
M	T	W	T	F	S	S
M	T	W	T	F	S	S
M	T	W	T	F	S	S
M	T	W	T	F	S	S

PRAYER LIST

OCT & NOV

MONDAY 26	TUESDAY 27	WEDNESDAY 28

NOTES

29 THURSDAY	30 FRIDAY	PRIORITIES

TO DO LIST

31 SATURDAY	1 SUNDAY
	All Saints

WEEKLY RETREAT • NOVEMBER 8, 2020

READING 1	READING 2	GOSPEL
Wisdom 6:12-16	1 Thessalonians 4:13-18	Matthew 25:1-13

"Then the kingdom of heaven will be like ten virgins who took their lamps and went out to meet the bridegroom. Five of them were foolish and five were wise. The foolish ones, when taking their lamps, brought no oil with them, but the wise brought flasks of oil with their lamps.

Matthew 25:1-4

REFLECTION

HOW WERE YOU IN AWE OF GOD THIS WEEK?

WEEKLY RETREAT

FREE SPACE

HABITS & RITUALS

M	T	W	T	F	S	S
M	T	W	T	F	S	S
M	T	W	T	F	S	S
M	T	W	T	F	S	S
M	T	W	T	F	S	S

PRAYER LIST

11 NOVEMBER

MONDAY 2
All Souls' Day

TUESDAY 3
Election Day

WEDNESDAY 4

NOTES

THURSDAY 5

FRIDAY 6

PRIORITIES

TO DO LIST

- [ ]
- [ ]
- [ ]
- [ ]
- [ ]
- [ ]
- [ ]
- [ ]
- [ ]
- [ ]
- [ ]
- [ ]
- [ ]
- [ ]
- [ ]
- [ ]
- [ ]
- [ ]
- [ ]
- [ ]
- [ ]
- [ ]
- [ ]
- [ ]

SATURDAY 7

SUNDAY 8

WEEKLY RETREAT • NOVEMBER 15, 2020

READING 1	READING 2	GOSPEL
Prv 31:10-13, 19-20, 30-31	1 Thessalonians 5:1-6	Matthew 25:14-30

The one who had received five talents came forward bringing the additional five. He said, 'Master, you gave me five talents. See, I have made five more.' His master said to him, 'Well done, my good and faithful servant. Since you were faithful in small matters, I will give you great responsibilities. Come, share your master's joy.'

Matthew 25:20-21

REFLECTION

HOW WERE YOU IN AWE OF GOD THIS WEEK?

WEEKLY RETREAT

FREE SPACE

HABITS & RITUALS

M	T	W	T	F	S	S
M	T	W	T	F	S	S
M	T	W	T	F	S	S
M	T	W	T	F	S	S
M	T	W	T	F	S	S

PRAYER LIST

NOVEMBER 11

MONDAY 9	TUESDAY 10	WEDNESDAY 11
		Veterans Day
		Rememberance Day (CA)

NOTES

THURSDAY 12	FRIDAY 13	PRIORITIES

TO DO LIST

SATURDAY 14	SUNDAY 15

WEEKLY RETREAT • NOVEMBER 22, 2020

READING 1	READING 2	GOSPEL
Ezekiel 34:11-12, 15-17	1 Corinthians 15:20-26, 28	Matthew 25:31-46

"When the Son of Man comes in his glory, and all the angels with him, he will sit upon his glorious throne, and all the nations will be assembled before him. And he will separate them one from another, as a shepherd separates the sheep from the goats.

Matthew 25:31-32

REFLECTION

HOW WERE YOU IN AWE OF GOD THIS WEEK?

WEEKLY RETREAT

FREE SPACE

HABITS & RITUALS

M	T	W	T	F	S	S
M	T	W	T	F	S	S
M	T	W	T	F	S	S
M	T	W	T	F	S	S
M	T	W	T	F	S	S

PRAYER LIST

11	NOVEMBER		
	16 MONDAY	**17** TUESDAY	**18** WEDNESDAY

NOTES

THURSDAY 19	FRIDAY 20	PRIORITIES

TO DO LIST

SATURDAY 21	SUNDAY 22
	Our Lord Jesus Christ, King of the Universe

WEEKLY RETREAT • NOVEMBER 29, 2020

READING 1	READING 2	GOSPEL
Is 63:16b-17, 19b; 64:2-7	1 Corinthians 1:3-9	Mark 13:33-37

Watch, therefore; you do not know when the lord of the house is coming, whether in the evening, or at midnight, or at cockcrow, or in the morning. May he not come suddenly and find you sleeping. What I say to you, I say to all: 'Watch!'"

Mark 13:35-37

REFLECTION

HOW WERE YOU IN AWE OF GOD THIS WEEK?

WEEKLY RETREAT

FREE SPACE

HABITS & RITUALS	PRAYER LIST
M T W T F S S	
M T W T F S S	
M T W T F S S	
M T W T F S S	
M T W T F S S	

11 NOVEMBER

23 MONDAY	24 TUESDAY	25 WEDNESDAY

NOTES

THURSDAY 26
Thanksgiving

FRIDAY 27

PRIORITIES

TO DO LIST

SATURDAY 28

SUNDAY 29

DECEMBER	SUNDAY	MONDAY	TUESDAY
NOTES			1
	6 Second Sunday of Advent	7 Saint Ambrose	8 **The Immaculate Conception of the Blessed Virgin Mary**
	13 Third Sunday of Advent	14 Saint John of the Cross	15
	20 Fourth Sunday of Advent	21 Saint Peter Canisius	22
	27 The Holy Family of Jesus, Mary & Joseph	28 The Holy Innocents	29 Saint Thomas Becket

SAINT EULALIA OF MÉRIDA

- Feast Day: December 10
- Born: 290; Died: 304
- Patron saint of Mérida, Spain; runaways, torture victims, widows, and inclement weather
- At the age of 12, Eulalia protested against the rulers for forcing the citizens of Mérida to worship false gods.
- Judge Dacian tried to flatter and bribe her, but she would not deny her faith.
- Eulalia was then tortured with hooks and torches and burned at the stake.
- Eulalia taunted her torturers while being burned and when she died, a dove flew out of her mouth. Then snow began to cover her body.

WEDNESDAY	THURSDAY	FRIDAY	SATURDAY
2	3 Saint Francis Xavier	4 Saint John Damascene	5
9 Saint Juan Diego Cuauhtlatoatzin	10 Saint Eulalia of Mérida	11 Saint Damasus I	12 Our Lady of Guadalupe
16	17	18	19
23 Saint John of Kanty	24	25 **The Nativity of the Lord, Christmas**	26 *Boxing Day (CA)* Saint Stephen
30	31 Saint Sylvester I		

GOALS

WEEKLY RETREAT • DECEMBER 6, 2020

READING 1	READING 2	GOSPEL
Isaiah 40:1-5, 9-11	2 Peter 3:8-14	Mark 1:1-8

John was clothed in camel's hair, with a leather belt around his waist. He fed on locusts and wild honey. And this is what he proclaimed: "One mightier than I is coming after me. I am not worthy to stoop and loosen the thongs of his sandals. I have baptized you with water; he will baptize you with the holy Spirit."

Mark:1:6-8

REFLECTION

HOW WERE YOU IN AWE OF GOD THIS WEEK?

WEEKLY RETREAT

FREE SPACE

HABITS & RITUALS							PRAYER LIST
M	T	W	T	F	S	S	
M	T	W	T	F	S	S	
M	T	W	T	F	S	S	
M	T	W	T	F	S	S	
M	T	W	T	F	S	S	

30 MONDAY	1 TUESDAY	2 WEDNESDAY

NOTES

THURSDAY 3

FRIDAY 4

PRIORITIES

TO DO LIST

SATURDAY 5

SUNDAY 6

WEEKLY RETREAT • DECEMBER 13, 2020

READING 1	READING 2	GOSPEL
Isaiah 61:1-2a, 10-11	1 Thessalonians 5:16-24	John 1:6-8, 19-28

They asked him, "Why then do you baptize if you are not the Messiah or Elijah or the Prophet?" John answered them, "I baptize with water; but there is one among you whom you do not recognize, the one who is coming after me, whose sandal strap I am not worthy to untie."

John 1:25-27

REFLECTION

HOW WERE YOU IN AWE OF GOD THIS WEEK?

WEEKLY RETREAT

FREE SPACE

HABITS & RITUALS

M	T	W	T	F	S	S
M	T	W	T	F	S	S
M	T	W	T	F	S	S
M	T	W	T	F	S	S
M	T	W	T	F	S	S

PRAYER LIST

12 DECEMBER

MONDAY 7	TUESDAY 8	WEDNESDAY 9
	The Immaculate Conception of the Blessed Virgin Mary	

NOTES

THURSDAY 10	FRIDAY 11	PRIORITIES

TO DO LIST

SATURDAY 12	SUNDAY 13

WEEKLY RETREAT • DECEMBER 20, 2020

READING 1	READING 2	GOSPEL
2 Sm 7:1-5, 8b-12, 14a, 16	Romans 16:25-27	Luke 1:26-38

And coming to her, he said, "Hail, favored one! The Lord is with you." But she was greatly troubled at what was said and pondered what sort of greeting this might be. Then the angel said to her, "Do not be afraid, Mary, for you have found favor with God.

Luke 1:28-30

REFLECTION

HOW WERE YOU IN AWE OF GOD THIS WEEK?

WEEKLY RETREAT

FREE SPACE

HABITS & RITUALS

M	T	W	T	F	S	S
M	T	W	T	F	S	S
M	T	W	T	F	S	S
M	T	W	T	F	S	S
M	T	W	T	F	S	S

PRAYER LIST

12 — DECEMBER

14 MONDAY	15 TUESDAY	16 WEDNESDAY

NOTES

THURSDAY 17

FRIDAY 18

PRIORITIES

TO DO LIST

SATURDAY 19

SUNDAY 20

WEEKLY RETREAT • DECEMBER 27, 2020

READING 1	READING 2	GOSPEL
Sirach 3:2-6, 12-14	Colossians 3:12-21	Luke 2:22-40

Now there was a man in Jerusalem whose name was Simeon. This man was righteous and devout, awaiting the consolation of Israel, and the holy Spirit was upon him. It had been revealed to him by the holy Spirit that he should not see death before he had seen the Messiah of the Lord.

Luke 2:25-26

REFLECTION

HOW WERE YOU IN AWE OF GOD THIS WEEK?

WEEKLY RETREAT

FREE SPACE

HABITS & RITUALS

M	T	W	T	F	S	S
M	T	W	T	F	S	S
M	T	W	T	F	S	S
M	T	W	T	F	S	S
M	T	W	T	F	S	S

PRAYER LIST

12 | DECEMBER

21 MONDAY	22 TUESDAY	23 WEDNESDAY

NOTES

THURSDAY 24

FRIDAY 25
The Nativity of the Lord, Christmas

PRIORITIES

TO DO LIST

SATURDAY 26
Boxing Day (CA)

SUNDAY 27

JANUARY	SUNDAY	MONDAY	TUESDAY
NOTES			
	3 The Epiphany of the Lord	4 Saint Elizabeth Ann Seton	5 Saint John Neumann
	10 The Baptism of the Lord	11	12
	17 Second Sunday in Ordinary Time	18 *Martin Luther King, Jr. Day*	19
	24 Third Sunday in Ordinary Time	25 The Conversion of Saint Paul the Apostle	26
	31 Fourth Sunday in Ordinary Time		

SAINT SEBASTIAN

- Feast Day: January 20
- Born: 256; Died: 288
- Patron saint of soldiers and athletes
- He served in the Roman army to assist other Christians being persecuted by the Romans.
- He was promoted to the Praetorian Guard to protect Emperor Diocletian.
- Twin deacons were arrested for refusing to make public sacrifices. Their parents tried to persuade them to renounce Christianity. Sebastian then converted the parents.
- Sebastian was ordered to be killed by being tied to a post and shot with arrows, but survived.
- He warned Diocletian of his sins and was killed.

WEDNESDAY	THURSDAY	FRIDAY	SATURDAY
		1 **Solemnity of Mary, the Holy Mother of God** *New Year's Day*	2 Saints Basil the Great & Gregory Nazianzen
6 Saint André Bessette	7 Saint Raymond of Penyafort	8	9
13 Saint Hilary	14	15	16
20 Saint Fabian Saint Sebastian	21 Saint Agnes	22 Day of Prayer for the Legal Protection of Unborn Children	23 Saint Vincent Saint Marianne Cope
27 Saint Angela Merici	28 Saint Thomas Aquinas	29	30

GOALS

WEEKLY RETREAT • JANUARY 3, 2021

READING 1	READING 2	GOSPEL
Isaiah 60:1-6	Ephesians 3:2-3a, 5-6	Matthew 2:1-12

They were overjoyed at seeing the star, and on entering the house they saw the child with Mary his mother. They prostrated themselves and did him homage. Then they opened their treasures and offered him gifts of gold, frankincense, and myrrh.

Matthew 2:10-11

REFLECTION

HOW WERE YOU IN AWE OF GOD THIS WEEK?

WEEKLY RETREAT

FREE SPACE

HABITS & RITUALS	PRAYER LIST

S M T W T F S

S M T W T F S

S M T W T F S

S M T W T F S

S M T W T F S

DEC & JAN

28 MONDAY	29 TUESDAY	30 WEDNESDAY

NOTES

THURSDAY 31	FRIDAY 1
	Solemnity of Mary, the Holy Mother of God *New Year's Day*

PRIORITIES

TO DO LIST

SATURDAY 2	SUNDAY 3

WEEKLY RETREAT • JANUARY 10, 2021

READING 1	READING 2	GOSPEL
Isaiah 42:1-4, 6-7	Acts 10:34-38	Mark 1:7-11

It happened in those days that Jesus came from Nazareth of Galilee and was baptized in the Jordan by John. On coming up out of the water he saw the heavens being torn open and the Spirit, like a dove, descending upon him. And a voice came from the heavens, "You are my beloved Son; with you I am well pleased."

Mark 1:9-11

REFLECTION

HOW WERE YOU IN AWE OF GOD THIS WEEK?

WEEKLY RETREAT

FREE SPACE

HABITS & RITUALS

S	M	T	W	T	F	S
S	M	T	W	T	F	S
S	M	T	W	T	F	S
S	M	T	W	T	F	S
S	M	T	W	T	F	S

PRAYER LIST

1 JANUARY

4 MONDAY	5 TUESDAY	6 WEDNESDAY

NOTES

THURSDAY 7	FRIDAY 8	PRIORITIES

TO DO LIST

SATURDAY 9	SUNDAY 10

WEEKLY RETREAT • JANUARY 17, 2021

READING 1	READING 2	GOSPEL
1 Samuel 3:3b-10, 19	1 Cor 6:13c-15a, 17-20	John 1:35-42

The next day John was there again with two of his disciples, and as he watched Jesus walk by, he said, "Behold, the Lamb of God." The two disciples heard what he said and followed Jesus.

John 1:35-37

REFLECTION

HOW WERE YOU IN AWE OF GOD THIS WEEK?

WEEKLY RETREAT

FREE SPACE

HABITS & RITUALS

S	M	T	W	T	F	S
S	M	T	W	T	F	S
S	M	T	W	T	F	S
S	M	T	W	T	F	S
S	M	T	W	T	F	S

PRAYER LIST

1 JANUARY

	MONDAY 11	TUESDAY 12	WEDNESDAY 13

NOTES

THURSDAY 14

FRIDAY 15

PRIORITIES

TO DO LIST

SATURDAY 16

SUNDAY 17

WEEKLY RETREAT • JANUARY 24, 2021

READING 1	READING 2	GOSPEL
Jonah 3:1-5, 10	1 Corinthians 7:29-31	Mark 1:14-20

After John had been arrested, Jesus came to Galilee proclaiming the gospel of God: "This is the time of fulfillment. The kingdom of God is at hand. Repent, and believe in the gospel."

Mark 1:14-15

REFLECTION

HOW WERE YOU IN AWE OF GOD THIS WEEK?

WEEKLY RETREAT

FREE SPACE

HABITS & RITUALS

S	M	T	W	T	F	S
S	M	T	W	T	F	S
S	M	T	W	T	F	S
S	M	T	W	T	F	S
S	M	T	W	T	F	S

PRAYER LIST

1 JANUARY

18 MONDAY	19 TUESDAY	20 WEDNESDAY
Martin Luther King, Jr. Day		

NOTES

21 THURSDAY	22 FRIDAY	PRIORITIES

TO DO LIST

23 SATURDAY	24 SUNDAY

WEEKLY RETREAT • JANUARY 31, 2021

READING 1	READING 2	GOSPEL
Deuteronomy 18:15-20	1 Corinthians 7:32-35	Mark 1:21-28

The unclean spirit convulsed him and with a loud cry came out of him. All were amazed and asked one another, "What is this? A new teaching with authority. He commands even the unclean spirits and they obey him." His fame spread everywhere throughout the whole region of Galilee.

Mark 1:26-28

REFLECTION

HOW WERE YOU IN AWE OF GOD THIS WEEK?

WEEKLY RETREAT

FREE SPACE

HABITS & RITUALS

S	M	T	W	T	F	S
S	M	T	W	T	F	S
S	M	T	W	T	F	S
S	M	T	W	T	F	S
S	M	T	W	T	F	S

PRAYER LIST

1 JANUARY

	MONDAY 25	TUESDAY 26	WEDNESDAY 27

NOTES

28 THURSDAY	29 FRIDAY	PRIORITIES

TO DO LIST

30 SATURDAY	31 SUNDAY

FEBRUARY	SUNDAY	MONDAY	TUESDAY
NOTES		1	2 The Presentation of the Lord
	7 Fifth Sunday in Ordinary Time	8 Saint Jerome Emiliani Saint Josephine Bakhita	9
	14 Sixth Sunday in Ordinary Time *Valentine's Day*	15 *Presidents' Day*	16
	21 First Sunday of Lent	22 The Chair of Saint Peter the Apostle	23 Saint Polycarp
	28 Second Sunday of Lent		

SAINT DOROTHY

- Feast Day: February 6
- Born: c.279–290; Died: c.311
- Patron saint of brewers, brides, florists, gardeners, and newlyweds
- She suffered persecution under Emperor Diocletian and was tortured and sentenced to death.
- On her way to execution, a pagan lawyer mocked her by telling her to send fruits from Christ's garden that she would soon be in.
- She sent her headdress to him before her execution, which was found filled with fruits and roses.
- The pagan lawyer, Theophilus, then converted.

WEDNESDAY	THURSDAY	FRIDAY	SATURDAY
3 Saint Blaise Saint Ansgar	4	5 Saint Agatha	6 Saint Paul Miki & Companions Saint Dorothy
10 Saint Scholastica	11 Our Lady of Lourdes	12	13
17 Ash Wednesday	18	19	20
24	25	26	27

GOALS

WEEKLY RETREAT • FEBRUARY 7, 2021

READING 1	READING 2	GOSPEL
Job 7:1-4, 6-7	1 Cor 9:16-19, 22-23	Mark 1:29-39

He told them, "Let us go on to the nearby villages that I may preach there also. For this purpose have I come." So he went into their synagogues, preaching and driving out demons throughout the whole of Galilee.

Mark 1:38-39

REFLECTION

HOW WERE YOU IN AWE OF GOD THIS WEEK?

WEEKLY RETREAT

FREE SPACE

HABITS & RITUALS

S	M	T	W	T	F	S
S	M	T	W	T	F	S
S	M	T	W	T	F	S
S	M	T	W	T	F	S
S	M	T	W	T	F	S

PRAYER LIST

FEBRUARY

MONDAY 1	TUESDAY 2	WEDNESDAY 3

NOTES

THURSDAY 4	FRIDAY 5	PRIORITIES

TO DO LIST

SATURDAY 6	SUNDAY 7

WEEKLY RETREAT • FEBRUARY 14, 2021

READING 1	READING 2	GOSPEL
Leviticus 13:1-2, 44-46	1 Corinthians 10:31—11:1	Mark 1:40-45

The man went away and began to publicize the whole matter. He spread the report abroad so that it was impossible for Jesus to enter a town openly. He remained outside in deserted places, and people kept coming to him from everywhere.

Mark 1:45

REFLECTION

HOW WERE YOU IN AWE OF GOD THIS WEEK?

WEEKLY RETREAT

FREE SPACE

HABITS & RITUALS

S	M	T	W	T	F	S
S	M	T	W	T	F	S
S	M	T	W	T	F	S
S	M	T	W	T	F	S
S	M	T	W	T	F	S

PRAYER LIST

2 FEBRUARY

MONDAY 8	TUESDAY 9	WEDNESDAY 10

NOTES

THURSDAY 11

FRIDAY 12

PRIORITIES

TO DO LIST

SATURDAY 13

SUNDAY 14

Valentine's Day

WEEKLY RETREAT • FEBRUARY 21, 2021

READING 1	READING 2	GOSPEL
Genesis 9:8-15	1 Peter 3:18-22	Mark 1:12-15

At once the Spirit drove him out into the desert, and he remained in the desert for forty days, tempted by Satan. He was among wild beasts, and the angels ministered to him.

Mark 1:12-13

REFLECTION

HOW WERE YOU IN AWE OF GOD THIS WEEK?

WEEKLY RETREAT

FREE SPACE

HABITS & RITUALS

S	M	T	W	T	F	S
S	M	T	W	T	F	S
S	M	T	W	T	F	S
S	M	T	W	T	F	S
S	M	T	W	T	F	S

PRAYER LIST

FEBRUARY

MONDAY 15
Presidents' Day

TUESDAY 16

WEDNESDAY 17
Ash Wednesday

NOTES

18 THURSDAY	19 FRIDAY	PRIORITIES

TO DO LIST

20 SATURDAY	21 SUNDAY

WEEKLY RETREAT • FEBRUARY 28, 2021

READING 1	READING 2	GOSPEL
Gen 22:1-2, 9a, 10-13, 15-18	Romans 8:31b-34	Mark 9:2-10

After six days Jesus took Peter, James, and John and led them up a high mountain apart by themselves. And he was transfigured before them, and his clothes became dazzling white, such as no fuller on earth could bleach them.

Mark 9:2-3

REFLECTION

HOW WERE YOU IN AWE OF GOD THIS WEEK?

WEEKLY RETREAT

FREE SPACE

HABITS & RITUALS	PRAYER LIST

S	M	T	W	T	F	S
S	M	T	W	T	F	S
S	M	T	W	T	F	S
S	M	T	W	T	F	S
S	M	T	W	T	F	S

2 FEBRUARY

22 MONDAY	23 TUESDAY	24 WEDNESDAY

NOTES

THURSDAY 25	FRIDAY 26	PRIORITIES

TO DO LIST

SATURDAY 27	SUNDAY 28

MARCH	SUNDAY	MONDAY	TUESDAY
NOTES		1	2
	7 — Third Sunday of Lent	8 — Saint John of God	9 — Saint Frances of Rome
	14 — Fourth Sunday of Lent	15	16
	21 — Fifth Sunday of Lent — Saint Nicholas of Flüe	22	23 — Saint Turibius of Mogrovejo
	28 — Palm Sunday of the Passion of the Lord	29	30

SAINT NICHOLAS OF FLÜE

- Feast Day: March 21
- Born: c.1417-1421; Died: March 1487
- Patron saint of Switzerland
- He was a military leader who fought with a sword in one hard and a rosary in the other.
- After receiving a mystical vision of a lily eaten by a horse, he took up the life of a hermit.
- He is said to have survived for nineteen years with no food except for the Holy Eucharist.
- He was visited by those who sought spiritual council throughout Europe.
- His intervention in a conflict over the admission of Fribourg and Solothurn to the Swiss Confederation helped prevent civil war.

WEDNESDAY	THURSDAY	FRIDAY	SATURDAY
3 Saint Katharine Drexel	4 Saint Casimir	5	6
10	11	12	13
17 Saint Patrick	18 Saint Cyril of Jerusalem	19 Saint Joseph, Spouse of the Blessed Virgin Mary	20
24 The Annunciation of the Lord	25	26	27
31			

GOALS

WEEKLY RETREAT • MARCH 7, 2021

READING 1	READING 2	GOSPEL
Exodus 20:1-17	1 Corinthians 1:22-25	John 2:13-25

Jesus answered and said to them, "Destroy this temple and in three days I will raise it up." The Jews said, "This temple has been under construction for forty-six years, and you will raise it up in three days?" But he was speaking about the temple of his body.

John 2:19-21

REFLECTION

HOW WERE YOU IN AWE OF GOD THIS WEEK?

WEEKLY RETREAT

FREE SPACE

HABITS & RITUALS	PRAYER LIST

S M T W T F S

S M T W T F S

S M T W T F S

S M T W T F S

S M T W T F S

3 | MARCH

	1 MONDAY	2 TUESDAY	3 WEDNESDAY

NOTES

THURSDAY 4	FRIDAY 5	PRIORITIES

TO DO LIST

SATURDAY 6	SUNDAY 7

WEEKLY RETREAT • MARCH 14, 2021

READING 1	READING 2	GOSPEL
2 Chr 36:14-16, 19-23	Ephesians 2:4-10	John 3:14-21

For God so loved the world that he gave his only Son, so that everyone who believes in him might not perish but might have eternal life. For God did not send his Son into the world to condemn the world, but that the world might be saved through him.

John 3:16-17

REFLECTION

HOW WERE YOU IN AWE OF GOD THIS WEEK?

WEEKLY RETREAT

FREE SPACE

HABITS & RITUALS	PRAYER LIST
S M T W T F S	
S M T W T F S	
S M T W T F S	
S M T W T F S	
S M T W T F S	

3 — MARCH

MONDAY 8	TUESDAY 9	WEDNESDAY 10

NOTES

THURSDAY 11	FRIDAY 12	PRIORITIES

TO DO LIST

SATURDAY 13	SUNDAY 14

WEEKLY RETREAT • MARCH 21, 2021

READING 1	READING 2	GOSPEL
Jeremiah 31:31-34	Hebrews 5:7-9	John 12:20-33

Amen, amen, I say to you, unless a grain of wheat falls to the ground and dies, it remains just a grain of wheat; but if it dies, it produces much fruit. Whoever loves his life loses it, and whoever hates his life in this world will preserve it for eternal life.

John 12:24-25

REFLECTION

HOW WERE YOU IN AWE OF GOD THIS WEEK?

WEEKLY RETREAT

FREE SPACE

HABITS & RITUALS	PRAYER LIST

S M T W T F S

S M T W T F S

S M T W T F S

S M T W T F S

S M T W T F S

3 MARCH

MONDAY 15
TUESDAY 16
WEDNESDAY 17

NOTES

THURSDAY 18

FRIDAY 19

PRIORITIES

TO DO LIST

SATURDAY 20

SUNDAY 21

WEEKLY RETREAT • MARCH 28, 2021

READING 1	READING 2	GOSPEL
Isaiah 50:4-7	Philippians 2:6-11	Mark 14:1—15:47

Then Judas Iscariot, one of the Twelve, went off to the chief priests to hand him over to them. When they heard him they were pleased and promised to pay him money. Then he looked for an opportunity to hand him over.

Mark 14:10-11

REFLECTION

HOW WERE YOU IN AWE OF GOD THIS WEEK?

WEEKLY RETREAT

FREE SPACE

HABITS & RITUALS

S	M	T	W	T	F	S
S	M	T	W	T	F	S
S	M	T	W	T	F	S
S	M	T	W	T	F	S
S	M	T	W	T	F	S

PRAYER LIST

MARCH

22 MONDAY	23 TUESDAY	24 WEDNESDAY
		The Annunciation of the Lord

NOTES

THURSDAY 25

FRIDAY 26

PRIORITIES

TO DO LIST

SATURDAY 27

SUNDAY 28

Palm Sunday

APRIL	SUNDAY	MONDAY	TUESDAY
NOTES			
	4 Easter Sunday	5 The Dedication of the Basilica of Saint Mary Major	6 The Transfiguration of the Lord
	11 Second Sunday of Easter Saint Gemma Galgani	12	13 Saint Martin I
	18 Third Sunday of Easter	19	20
	25 Fourth Sunday of Easter	26	27

SAINT GEMMA GALGANI

- Feast Day: April 11
- Born: 1878; Died: April 11, 1903
- Patron saint of students, pharmacists, against temptation, and against loss of parents
- She was know as the "Flower of Lucca."
- She attended a Catholic boarding school and developed a love for prayer at a young age.
- She developed spinal meningitus at the age of 16 and prayed to the Sacred Heart of Jesus.
- At the age of 16, she became the mother figure to her younger siblings when her father died.
- She experienced stigmata at the age of 21.
- She often saw and spoke to her guardian angel, Jesus, Mary and other saints.

WEDNESDAY	THURSDAY	FRIDAY	SATURDAY
	1 Holy Thursday	2 Good Friday Saint Francis of Paola	3 Holy Saturday
7 Saint John Baptist de la Salle	8	9	10
14	15	16 Saint Bernadette	17
21 Saint Anselm	22	23 Saint George Saint Adalbert	24 Saint Fidelis of Sigmaringen
28 Saint Peter Chanel Saint Louis Mary de Montfort	29 Saint Catherine of Siena	30 Saint Pius V	

GOALS

WEEKLY RETREAT • APRIL 4, 2021

READING 1	READING 2	GOSPEL
Acts 10:34a, 37-43	Colossians 3:1-4	John 20:1-9

When Simon Peter arrived after him, he went into the tomb and saw the burial cloths there, and the cloth that had covered his head, not with the burial cloths but rolled up in a separate place. Then the other disciple also went in, the one who had arrived at the tomb first, and he saw and believed.

John 20:6-8

REFLECTION

HOW WERE YOU IN AWE OF GOD THIS WEEK?

WEEKLY RETREAT

FREE SPACE

HABITS & RITUALS

S	M	T	W	T	F	S
S	M	T	W	T	F	S
S	M	T	W	T	F	S
S	M	T	W	T	F	S
S	M	T	W	T	F	S

PRAYER LIST

MAR & APR

29 MONDAY	30 TUESDAY	31 WEDNESDAY

NOTES

THURSDAY 1

Holy Thursday

FRIDAY 2

Good Friday

PRIORITIES

TO DO LIST

SATURDAY 3

Holy Saturday

SUNDAY 4

Easter

WEEKLY RETREAT • APRIL 11, 2021

READING 1	READING 2	GOSPEL
Acts 4:32-35	1 John 5:1-6	John 20:19-31

Thomas, called Didymus, one of the Twelve, was not with them when Jesus came. So the other disciples said to him, "We have seen the Lord." But he said to them, "Unless I see the mark of the nails in his hands and put my finger into the nailmarks and put my hand into his side, I will not believe."

John 20:24-25

REFLECTION

HOW WERE YOU IN AWE OF GOD THIS WEEK?

WEEKLY RETREAT

FREE SPACE

HABITS & RITUALS

S	M	T	W	T	F	S
S	M	T	W	T	F	S
S	M	T	W	T	F	S
S	M	T	W	T	F	S
S	M	T	W	T	F	S

PRAYER LIST

4 APRIL

5 MONDAY	6 TUESDAY	7 WEDNESDAY

NOTES

THURSDAY 8	FRIDAY 9	PRIORITIES

TO DO LIST

SATURDAY 10	SUNDAY 11

WEEKLY RETREAT • APRIL 18, 2021

READING 1	READING 2	GOSPEL
Acts 3:13-15, 17-19	1 John 2:1-5a	Luke 24:35-48

After three days they found him in the temple, sitting in the midst of the teachers, listening to them and asking them questions, and all who heard him were astounded at his understanding and his answers.

Luke 2:46-47

REFLECTION

HOW WERE YOU IN AWE OF GOD THIS WEEK?

WEEKLY RETREAT

FREE SPACE

HABITS & RITUALS

S	M	T	W	T	F	S
S	M	T	W	T	F	S
S	M	T	W	T	F	S
S	M	T	W	T	F	S
S	M	T	W	T	F	S

PRAYER LIST

4 | APRIL

12 MONDAY	13 TUESDAY	14 WEDNESDAY

NOTES

THURSDAY 15	FRIDAY 16	PRIORITIES

TO DO LIST

SATURDAY 17	SUNDAY 18

WEEKLY RETREAT • APRIL 25, 2021

READING 1	READING 2	GOSPEL
Acts 4:8-12	1 John 3:1-2	John 10:11-18

I am the good shepherd. A good shepherd lays down his life for the sheep. A hired man, who is not a shepherd and whose sheep are not his own, sees a wolf coming and leaves the sheep and runs away, and the wolf catches and scatters them. This is because he works for pay and has no concern for the sheep.

John 10:11-13

REFLECTION

HOW WERE YOU IN AWE OF GOD THIS WEEK?

WEEKLY RETREAT

FREE SPACE

HABITS & RITUALS

S	M	T	W	T	F	S
S	M	T	W	T	F	S
S	M	T	W	T	F	S
S	M	T	W	T	F	S
S	M	T	W	T	F	S

PRAYER LIST

4 APRIL

19 MONDAY	20 TUESDAY	21 WEDNESDAY

NOTES

THURSDAY 22

FRIDAY 23

PRIORITIES

TO DO LIST

SATURDAY 24

SUNDAY 25

MAY	SUNDAY	MONDAY	TUESDAY
NOTES			
	2 — Fifth Sunday of Easter	3 — Saints Philip & James	4
	9 — Sixth Sunday of Easter / Mother's Day	10 — Saint Damien de Veuster	11
	16 — The Ascension of the Lord/ Seventh Sunday of Easter*	17	18 — Saint John I
	23 — Pentecost Sunday	24 — The Blessed Virgin Mary, Mother of the Church / Victoria Day (CA)	25
	30 — The Most Holy Trinity	31 — The Visitation of the Blessed Virgin Mary / Memorial Day	Saint Bede the Venerable / Saint Gregory VII / Saint Mary Magdalene de' Pazzi

SAINT MARY MAGDALENE DE' PAZZI

- Feast Day: May 27
- Born: April 2, 1566; Died: March 25, 1607
- Patron saint of sick people and against temptation
- She was born to one of the wealthiest noble families of Renaissance Florence.
- She took a vow of virginity at a young age.
- She experienced her first religious ecstasy at the age of 12 and continued to exhibit many mystical experiences thereafter.
- She was educated at a monastery of nuns.
- During her ecstasies, she dictated her experiences to her fellow nuns and filled five large books over six years.

WEDNESDAY	THURSDAY	FRIDAY	SATURDAY
			1 Saint Joseph the Worker
5	6	7	8
12 Saints Nereus & Achilleus Saint Pancras	13 The Ascension of the Lord*	14 Saint Matthias	15 Saint Isidore Saint Dymphna
19	20 Saint Bernadine of Siena	21 Saint Christopher Magallanes & Companions	22 Saint Rita of Cascia
26 Saint Philip Neri	27 Saint Augustine of Canterbury Saint Mary Magdalene de' Pazzi	28	29 Saint Paul VI

*Ecclesiastical Provinces of Boston, Hartford, New York, Newark, Omaha, Philadelphia

GOALS

WEEKLY RETREAT • MAY 2, 2021

READING 1	READING 2	GOSPEL
Acts 9:26-31	1 John 3:18-24	John 15:1-8

Remain in me, as I remain in you. Just as a branch cannot bear fruit on its own unless it remains on the vine, so neither can you unless you remain in me. I am the vine, you are the branches. Whoever remains in me and I in him will bear much fruit, because without me you can do nothing.

John 15:4-5

REFLECTION

HOW WERE YOU IN AWE OF GOD THIS WEEK?

WEEKLY RETREAT

FREE SPACE

HABITS & RITUALS							PRAYER LIST
S	M	T	W	T	F	S	
S	M	T	W	T	F	S	
S	M	T	W	T	F	S	
S	M	T	W	T	F	S	
S	M	T	W	T	F	S	

APR & MAY

	MONDAY 26	TUESDAY 27	WEDNESDAY 28

NOTES

THURSDAY 29	FRIDAY 30	PRIORITIES

TO DO LIST

SATURDAY 1	SUNDAY 2

WEEKLY RETREAT • MAY 9, 2021

READING 1	READING 2	GOSPEL
Acts 10:25-26, 34-35, 44-48	1 John 4:7-10	John 15:9-17

As the Father loves me, so I also love you. Remain in my love. If you keep my commandments, you will remain in my love, just as I have kept my Father's commandments and remain in his love. I have told you this so that my joy may be in you and your joy may be complete. This is my commandment: love one another as I love you.

John 15:9-12

REFLECTION

HOW WERE YOU IN AWE OF GOD THIS WEEK?

WEEKLY RETREAT

FREE SPACE

HABITS & RITUALS

S	M	T	W	T	F	S
S	M	T	W	T	F	S
S	M	T	W	T	F	S
S	M	T	W	T	F	S
S	M	T	W	T	F	S

PRAYER LIST

_____

_____

_____

_____

_____

5 | MAY

3 MONDAY	4 TUESDAY	5 WEDNESDAY

NOTES

	THURSDAY		FRIDAY	PRIORITIES

6 / 7

TO DO LIST

	SATURDAY		SUNDAY

8 / 9

Mother's Day

WEEKLY RETREAT • MAY 16, 2021

READING 1	READING 2	GOSPEL
Acts 1:1-11	Ephesians 1:17-23	Mark 16:15-20

These signs will accompany those who believe: in my name they will drive out demons, they will speak new languages. They will pick up serpents [with their hands], and if they drink any deadly thing, it will not harm them. They will lay hands on the sick, and they will recover."

Mark 16:17-18

REFLECTION

HOW WERE YOU IN AWE OF GOD THIS WEEK?

WEEKLY RETREAT

FREE SPACE

HABITS & RITUALS

S	M	T	W	T	F	S
S	M	T	W	T	F	S
S	M	T	W	T	F	S
S	M	T	W	T	F	S
S	M	T	W	T	F	S

PRAYER LIST

5 | MAY

10 MONDAY	11 TUESDAY	12 WEDNESDAY

NOTES

THURSDAY	FRIDAY	PRIORITIES
13	14	
The Ascension of the Lord*		

TO DO LIST

SATURDAY	SUNDAY
15	16
	The Ascension of the Lord

WEEKLY RETREAT • MAY 23, 2021

READING 1	READING 2	GOSPEL
Genesis 11:1-9	Romans 8:22-27	John 7:37-39

On the last and greatest day of the feast, Jesus stood up and exclaimed, "Let anyone who thirsts come to me and drink.
Whoever believes in me, as scripture says:
'Rivers of living water will flow from within him.'"

John 7:37-38

REFLECTION

HOW WERE YOU IN AWE OF GOD THIS WEEK?

WEEKLY RETREAT

FREE SPACE

HABITS & RITUALS

S	M	T	W	T	F	S
S	M	T	W	T	F	S
S	M	T	W	T	F	S
S	M	T	W	T	F	S
S	M	T	W	T	F	S

PRAYER LIST

5 | MAY

17 MONDAY	18 TUESDAY	19 WEDNESDAY

NOTES

THURSDAY 20

FRIDAY 21

PRIORITIES

TO DO LIST

SATURDAY 22

SUNDAY 23

Pentecost

WEEKLY RETREAT • MAY 30, 2021

READING 1	READING 2	GOSPEL
Dt 4:32-34, 39-40	Romans 8:14-17	Matthew 28:16-20

Then Jesus approached and said to them, "All power in heaven and on earth has been given to me. Go, therefore and make disciples of all nations, baptizing them in the name of the Father, and of the Son, and of the holy Spirit, teaching them to observe all that I have commanded you. And behold, I am with you always, until the end of the age."

Matthew 28:18-20

REFLECTION

HOW WERE YOU IN AWE OF GOD THIS WEEK?

WEEKLY RETREAT

FREE SPACE

HABITS & RITUALS

S	M	T	W	T	F	S
S	M	T	W	T	F	S
S	M	T	W	T	F	S
S	M	T	W	T	F	S
S	M	T	W	T	F	S

PRAYER LIST

5 — MAY

MONDAY 24
Victoria Day (CA)

TUESDAY 25

WEDNESDAY 26

NOTES

THURSDAY 27

FRIDAY 28

PRIORITIES

TO DO LIST

SATURDAY 29

SUNDAY 30

The Most Holy Trinity

JUNE	SUNDAY	MONDAY	TUESDAY
NOTES			1 Saint Justin
	6 — The Most Holy Body and Blood of Christ	7 — The Dedication of the Basilica of Saint Mary Major	8 — The Transfiguration of the Lord
	13 — Eleventh Sunday in Ordinary Time	14	15
	20 — Twelfth Sunday in Ordinary Time *Father's Day*	21 Saint Aloysius Gonzaga	22 Saint Paulinus of Nola Saints John Fisher & Thomas More
	27 — Thirteenth Sunday in Ordinary Time	28 Saint Irenaeus	29 Saints Peter & Paul

SAINT JUSTIN

- Feast Day: June 1
- Born: 100; Died: 165
- Patron saint of philosophers
- He was an early Christian apologist, who defended the Christian religion in writing.
- He studied many different schools of philosophy, but was left unsatisfied.
- He encountered an old man who convinced him that the testimony of the prophets were more reliable than the reasoning of philosophers.
- Most of his works are lost, but two apologies and a dialogue did survive.
- He was martyred along side some of his students.

WEDNESDAY	THURSDAY	FRIDAY	SATURDAY
2 Saints Marcellinus & Peter	3 Saint Charles Lwanga & Companions	4	5 Saint Boniface
9 Saint Ephrem	10	11 The Most Sacred Heart of Jesus Saint Barnabas	12 The Immaculate Heart of the Blessed Virgin Mary
16	17	18	19 Saint Romuald
23	24 The Nativity of Saint John the Baptist	25	26
30 The First Martyrs of the Holy Roman Church			

GOALS

WEEKLY RETREAT • JUNE 6, 2021

READING 1	READING 2	GOSPEL
Exodus 24:3-8	Hebrews 9:11-15	Mark 14:12-16, 22-26

He said to them, "This is my blood of the covenant, which will be shed for many. Amen, I say to you, I shall not drink again the fruit of the vine until the day when I drink it new in the kingdom of God."

Mark 14:24-25

REFLECTION

HOW WERE YOU IN AWE OF GOD THIS WEEK?

WEEKLY RETREAT

FREE SPACE

HABITS & RITUALS

S	M	T	W	T	F	S

S	M	T	W	T	F	S

S	M	T	W	T	F	S

S	M	T	W	T	F	S

S	M	T	W	T	F	S

PRAYER LIST

MAY & JUN

31 MONDAY	1 TUESDAY	2 WEDNESDAY
Memorial Day		

NOTES

THURSDAY 3	FRIDAY 4	PRIORITIES

TO DO LIST

SATURDAY 5	SUNDAY 6

WEEKLY RETREAT • JUNE 13, 2021

READING 1	READING 2	GOSPEL
Exodus 24:3-8	Hebrews 9:11-15	Mark 4:26-34

He said, "This is how it is with the kingdom of God; it is as if a man were to scatter seed on the land and would sleep and rise night and day and the seed would sprout and grow, he knows not how.

Mark 4:26-27

REFLECTION

HOW WERE YOU IN AWE OF GOD THIS WEEK?

WEEKLY RETREAT

FREE SPACE

HABITS & RITUALS	PRAYER LIST
S M T W T F S	
S M T W T F S	
S M T W T F S	
S M T W T F S	
S M T W T F S	

6	JUNE		
	7 MONDAY	8 TUESDAY	9 WEDNESDAY

NOTES

THURSDAY 10

FRIDAY 11
The Most Sacred Heart of Jesus

PRIORITIES

TO DO LIST

SATURDAY 12

SUNDAY 13

WEEKLY RETREAT • JUNE 20, 2021

READING 1	READING 2	GOSPEL
Job 38:1, 8-11	2 Corinthians 5:14-17	Mark 4:35-41

Jesus was in the stern, asleep on a cushion. They woke him and said to him, "Teacher, do you not care that we are perishing?" He woke up, rebuked the wind, and said to the sea, "Quiet! Be still!" The wind ceased and there was great calm. Then he asked them, "Why are you terrified? Do you not yet have faith?"

Mark 4:38-40

REFLECTION

HOW WERE YOU IN AWE OF GOD THIS WEEK?

WEEKLY RETREAT

FREE SPACE

HABITS & RITUALS	PRAYER LIST

S	M	T	W	T	F	S
S	M	T	W	T	F	S
S	M	T	W	T	F	S
S	M	T	W	T	F	S
S	M	T	W	T	F	S

6	JUNE		
	14 MONDAY	**15** TUESDAY	**16** WEDNESDAY

NOTES

THURSDAY 17

FRIDAY 18

PRIORITIES

TO DO LIST

SATURDAY 19

SUNDAY 20

Father's Day

WEEKLY RETREAT • JUNE 27, 2021

READING 1	READING 2	GOSPEL
Wisdom 1:13-15, 2:23-24	2 Corinthians 8:7, 9, 13-15	Mark 5:21-43

One of the synagogue officials, named Jairus, came forward. Seeing him he fell at his feet and pleaded earnestly with him, saying, "My daughter is at the point of death. Please, come lay your hands on her that she may get well and live."

Mark 5:22-23

REFLECTION

HOW WERE YOU IN AWE OF GOD THIS WEEK?

WEEKLY RETREAT

FREE SPACE

HABITS & RITUALS	PRAYER LIST

S M T W T F S

S M T W T F S

S M T W T F S

S M T W T F S

S M T W T F S

6 JUNE

21 MONDAY	22 TUESDAY	23 WEDNESDAY

NOTES

THURSDAY 24

The Nativity of John the Baptist

FRIDAY 25

PRIORITIES

TO DO LIST

SATURDAY 26

SUNDAY 27

JULY	SUNDAY	MONDAY	TUESDAY
NOTES			
	4 Fourteenth Sunday in Ordinary Time *Independence Day*	5 The Dedication of the Basilica of Saint Mary Major	6 The Transfiguration of the Lord Saint Maria Goretti
	11 Fifteenth Sunday in Ordinary Time	12 Saint Jane Frances de Chantal	13 Saints Pontian & Hippolytus
	18 Sixteenth Sunday in Ordinary Time	19 Saint John Eudes	20 Saint Bernard
	25 Seventeenth Sunday in Ordinary Time	26	27 Saint Monica

SAINT MARIA GORETTI

- Feast Day: July 6
- Born: October 16, 1890; Died: July 6, 1902
- Patron saint of victims of rape, crime victims, teenage girls, and modern youth
- She was born into a farming family.
- When her dad died when she was 9, she took over household duties.
- An 18 year old neighbor tried to make sexual advances and lead her into sin.
- She refused the man and he stabbed her.
- She forgave her murderer before her death two days later.
- The man converted to Christianity in prison after a dream of Maria handing him lilies.

WEDNESDAY	THURSDAY	FRIDAY	SATURDAY
	1	2	3
	Saint Alphonsus Liguori	Saint Eusebius of Vercelli Saint Peter Julian Eymard	
7	8	9	10
Saint Sixtus II & Companions Saint Cajetan	Saint Dominic	Saint Teresa Benedicta of the Cross	Saint Lawrence
14	15	16	17
Saint Maximilian Kolbe		Saint Stephen of Hungary	
21	22	23	24
Saint Pius X		Saint Rose of Lima	Saint Bartholomew
28	29	30	31
Saint Augustine			

GOALS

WEEKLY RETREAT • JULY 4, 2021

READING 1	READING 2	GOSPEL
Ezekiel 2:2-5	2 Corinthians 12:7-10	Mark 6:1-6a

Is he not the carpenter, the son of Mary, and the brother of James and Joses and Judas and Simon? And are not his sisters here with us?" And they took offense at him. Jesus said to them, "A prophet is not without honor except in his native place and among his own kin and in his own house."

Mark 6:3-4

REFLECTION

HOW WERE YOU IN AWE OF GOD THIS WEEK?

WEEKLY RETREAT

FREE SPACE

HABITS & RITUALS

S	M	T	W	T	F	S
S	M	T	W	T	F	S
S	M	T	W	T	F	S
S	M	T	W	T	F	S
S	M	T	W	T	F	S

PRAYER LIST

JUN & JUL

MONDAY 28	TUESDAY 29	WEDNESDAY 30

NOTES

THURSDAY 1	FRIDAY 2	PRIORITIES

TO DO LIST

SATURDAY 3	SUNDAY 4
	Independence Day

WEEKLY RETREAT • JULY 11, 2021

READING 1	READING 2	GOSPEL
Amos 7:12-15	Ephesians 1:3-14	Mark 6:7-13

He said to them, "Wherever you enter a house, stay there until you leave from there. Whatever place does not welcome you or listen to you, leave there and shake the dust off your feet in testimony against them." So they went off and preached repentance.

Mark 6:10-12

REFLECTION

HOW WERE YOU IN AWE OF GOD THIS WEEK?

WEEKLY RETREAT

FREE SPACE

HABITS & RITUALS	PRAYER LIST

S M T W T F S

S M T W T F S

S M T W T F S

S M T W T F S

S M T W T F S

7 | JULY

	5 MONDAY	**6** TUESDAY	**7** WEDNESDAY

NOTES

THURSDAY 8	FRIDAY 9	PRIORITIES

TO DO LIST

SATURDAY 10	SUNDAY 11

WEEKLY RETREAT • JULY 18, 2021

READING 1	READING 2	GOSPEL
Jeremiah 23:1-6	Ephesians 2:13-18	Mark 6:30-34

When he disembarked and saw the vast crowd, his heart was moved with pity for them, for they were like sheep without a shepherd; and he began to teach them many things.

Mark 6:34

REFLECTION

HOW WERE YOU IN AWE OF GOD THIS WEEK?

WEEKLY RETREAT

FREE SPACE

HABITS & RITUALS

S	M	T	W	T	F	S
S	M	T	W	T	F	S
S	M	T	W	T	F	S
S	M	T	W	T	F	S
S	M	T	W	T	F	S

PRAYER LIST

7 | JULY

12 MONDAY	13 TUESDAY	14 WEDNESDAY

NOTES

THURSDAY 15

FRIDAY 16

PRIORITIES

TO DO LIST

SATURDAY 17

SUNDAY 18

WEEKLY RETREAT • JULY 25, 2021

READING 1	READING 2	GOSPEL
2 Kings 4:42-44	Ephesians 4:1-6	John 6:1-15

When Jesus raised his eyes and saw that a large crowd was coming to him, he said to Philip, "Where can we buy enough food for them to eat?" He said this to test him, because he himself knew what he was going to do. Philip answered him, "Two hundred days' wages worth of food would not be enough for each of them to have a little [bit]."

John 6:5-7

REFLECTION

HOW WERE YOU IN AWE OF GOD THIS WEEK?

WEEKLY RETREAT

FREE SPACE

HABITS & RITUALS

| S | M | T | W | T | F | S |

| S | M | T | W | T | F | S |

| S | M | T | W | T | F | S |

| S | M | T | W | T | F | S |

| S | M | T | W | T | F | S |

PRAYER LIST

7 JULY

19 MONDAY	20 TUESDAY	21 WEDNESDAY

NOTES

| THURSDAY 22 | FRIDAY 23 | PRIORITIES |

TO DO LIST

| SATURDAY 24 | SUNDAY 25 |

WEEKLY RETREAT • AUGUST 1, 2021

READING 1	READING 2	GOSPEL
Exodus 16:2-4, 12-15	Ephesians 4:17, 20-24	John 6:24-35

Jesus answered them and said, "Amen, amen, I say to you, you are looking for me not because you saw signs but because you ate the loaves and were filled. Do not work for food that perishes but for the food that endures for eternal life, which the Son of Man will give you. For on him the Father, God, has set his seal."

John 6:26-27

REFLECTION

HOW WERE YOU IN AWE OF GOD THIS WEEK?

WEEKLY RETREAT

FREE SPACE

HABITS & RITUALS	PRAYER LIST
S M T W T F S	
S M T W T F S	
S M T W T F S	
S M T W T F S	
S M T W T F S	

JUL & AUG

	MONDAY 26	TUESDAY 27	WEDNESDAY 28

NOTES

29 THURSDAY	30 FRIDAY	PRIORITIES

TO DO LIST

31 SATURDAY	1 SUNDAY

YEAR END REVIEW

Congratulations! You made it through the school year!
Look back at your Path to Sainthood and reflect on the year you accomplished.

Scripture texts in this work are taken from the *New American Bible, revised edition* © 2010, 1991, 1986, 1970 Confraternity of Christian Doctrine, Washington, D.C. and are used by permission of the copyright owner. All Rights Reserved. No part of the New American Bible may be reproduced in any form without permission in writing from the copyright owner.